"Why"
Sermon Outlines

Russell E. Spray

Baker Books

A Division of Baker Book House Co
Grand Rapids, Michigan 49516

© 1980 by Baker Book House Company

Published by Baker Books
a division of Baker Book House Company
P.O. Box 6287, Grand Rapids, MI 49516-6287

New paperback edition published 2001

Printed in the United States of America

ISBN 0-8010-9131-4

For current information about all releases from Baker Book House, visit our web site:
http://www.bakerbooks.com

CONTENTS

1

WHY Christ Brings Meaning to L-I-F-E

"I am come that they might have life, and that they might have it more abundantly" (John 10:10).

I. **L-ove (Loving Through Christ)**
"Beloved, if God so loved us, we ought also to love one another" (I John 4:11).
   A. Life has little meaning to some because they possess so little love. Christ loved us and died for us, paying the penalty for our sins. When Christ is Lord of our life, He should be the love of our life also.
   B. Christ's love brings meaning to our life. His love must reach out through us to help, comfort, and share Christ with others (Matt. 28:19).

II. **I-nstruction (Learning from Christ)**
"I will instruct thee and teach thee in the way which thou shalt go: I will guide thee with mine eye" (Ps. 32:8).
   A. When we are forgiven, cleansed, and filled with the love of Christ, we have just begun to live. We still have much to learn. We will continue to face frustrations and possible failure.
   B. We must depend on Christ's Holy Spirit for guidance and direction. He will help us through frustration and will bring victory and meaning to life as we keep on praying, learning from His Word, trusting, and obeying (John 14:26).

III. **F-reedom (Liberty in Christ)**
"Stand fast therefore in the liberty wherewith Christ hath made us free..." (Gal. 5:1).
   A. Many are bound by sinful pleasures, social pressures, and sensual practices. They are in bondage to themselves, others, and Satan. Life has little meaning.
   B. Christ came to bring freedom from the bondage of sin. He breaks the fetters that bind and sets free all who come to Him in repentance and faith.

C. Christians are liberated and their lives become meaningful. When one's sins are forgiven, one's heart is cleansed. One is free to help others find their way to heaven (John 8:36).

IV. **E-ternal Life (Living with Christ)**
"...God hath given to us eternal life, and this life is in his Son" (I John 5:11).
   A. Everyone wants to live. But only those who have accepted Christ as Saviour and Lord will live eternally.
   B. Life here on earth is brief at best. We should make the most of it. This life can have real meaning only if we are prepared for the next life.
   C. Christians look forward with anticipation to living forever with Christ. He has gone to prepare a place for them. He has promised to return and receive them unto Himself (John 14:1–3).

2

WHY Christ Is Crowded Out (Christmas)

"...there was no room for them in the inn" (Luke 2:7).

Introduction: Christ was crowded out when He came to this earth to be the Saviour of mankind. He is crowded out today in different, but just as real, ways.

I. **Social Pressures**
"Having a form of godliness, but denying the power thereof" (II Tim. 3:5).
   A. Many fail to take their stand for God because of social pressures. They give in to Satan for fear of losing their position or popularity.
   B. We must give Christ first place in our lives and not allow social pressures to crowd Him out.

C. If we are fearless, faithful, and fruitful for Him, He will be our helper, guide, and "a friend that sticketh closer than a brother" (Prov. 18:24).

II. Secular Pleasures

"...lovers of pleasures more than lovers of God" (II Tim. 3:4).

A. We live in a pleasure-mad world. Millions are seeking something to satisfy the longing and emptiness in their lives and souls (Ps. 107:9).

B. Worldly pleasures do not bring real joy and contentment. They crowd out the Christ who can give true happiness and satisfaction, leaving an inner void and disappointment.

C. Christ gives lasting pleasure to those who accept Him as Saviour and Lord of their lives.

III. Sensual Passions

"...led away with divers lusts" (II Tim. 3:6).

A. Immoral standards have crowded Christ out of millions of lives. Illicit sex, including adultery, homosexuality, etc., have invaded and polluted the world.

B. God's promises never fail. He has promised to judge those who commit such sins.

C. Prayer and faith help Christians to live pure and holy lives and to be temples of the Holy Spirit (I Cor. 6:19).

IV. Selfish Pursuits

"For men shall be lovers of their own selves, covetous, boasters, proud..." (II Tim. 3:2).

A. Temporal possessions are crowding Christ out of the lives of millions. The pursuit of earthly wealth is consuming lives and love.

B. We must give Christ prime time and first place in our lives. We must love Him with all our heart, mind, soul, and strength (Luke 10:27).

C. Making room for Christ means loving our neighbor (Luke 10:27). We must help the less fortunate, comfort the lonely, and share Christ with the unsaved.

3

WHY Christians Are Called to Commitment

"Who hath saved us, and called us with an holy calling, not according to our works, but according to his own purpose and grace..."(II Tim. 1:9).

I. Christians Are Called Out
"Wherefore come out from among them, and be ye separate, saith the Lord..." (II Cor. 6:17).
- A. Some try to hold on to God with one hand and to sin and the world with the other. This is impossible to do; we cannot serve God and Satan at the same time (Matt. 6:24).
- B. Christians are called out of the old life of sin—the love of money, the lust for illicit sex, living for pleasure and popularity.
- C. They love God's presence, purpose, and people. They are separated from the Lord.

II. Christians Are Called In
"Therefore if any man be in Christ, he is a new creature" (II Cor. 5:17).
- A. Christ died on the cross to bring mankind back into fellowship with God. All who accept Him as Lord of their lives become new creatures in Christ.
- B. Christians are called into service for the Lord. They should feel compassion for others, help the needy, and witness to the lost as opportunity affords.
- C. Christians should want others to become new creatures in Christ.

III. Christians Are Called Down
"...hereunto were ye called: because Christ also suffered for us, leaving us an example, that ye should follow his steps" (I Peter 2:21).
- A. Christians are sometimes called down into the valley of suffering and sorrow, testing and trial, perplexity and persecution (II Tim. 3:12).

B. God always has a purpose in what He allows. It may be to teach patience, to test faith, to testify to others, or to train for service.

C. God has special help for Christians who are called to go down into the valley. They should not be afraid, for God is with them (Ps. 23:4).

IV. **Christians Will Be Called Up**

"Then we...shall be caught up together with them in the clouds, to meet the Lord...and so shall we ever be with the Lord" (I Thess. 4:17).

A. Throughout the centuries Christians have looked forward to eternal life with Christ in their heavenly home.

B. All the beauty of the earth was created in only six days. Christ has been preparing a place for those who love Him. He has been working at it for nearly two thousand years.

C. It is little wonder that in reference to our heavenly home the Scripture says, "Eye hath not seen, nor ear heard, neither have entered into the heart of man, the things which God hath prepared for them that love him" (I Cor. 2:9).

4

WHY Christians Are Tested

"That the trial of your faith, being much more precious than of gold that perisheth, though it be tried with fire, might be found unto praise and honour and glory at the appearing of Jesus Christ" (I Peter 1:7).

I. **To Increase Their Surrender**

"Before I was afflicted I went astray: but now have I kept thy word" (Ps. 119:67).

A. Christians are sometimes afflicted in order to encourage their surrender to God and to bring them closer to Him.

9

B. Some Christians become spiritually lean and go astray when everything is going well. They depend on their own strength and resources.

C. We must depend on God's help daily. We must keep in constant fellowship with Him through prayer, Bible reading, and faithful attendance to the means of grace (I Thess. 5:17–23).

II. To Insure Their Stability

"...after that ye have suffered a while, make you perfect, stablish, strengthen, settle you" (I Peter 5:10).

A. Some Christians are unstable and undependable. They are up and down and run from place to place.

B. Troubles, trials, and temptations may cause a Christian to become temporarily unstable. If they maintain their devotion to God, He will establish, strengthen, and settle them.

C. When testing strikes, we should look for the reason and learn the lesson God is trying to teach. God always has a purpose in what He allows (Rom. 8:28).

III. To Inspire Others Who Struggle

"And many...waxing confident by my bonds, are much more bold to speak the word without fear" (Phil. 1:14).

A. Paul was imprisoned for preaching Christ with boldness. Because he endured bravely when tested, others were inspired to speak the Word of God fearlessly.

B. God allows Christians today to be tested in order to inspire others. He places confidence in them, for testing is proof of their faith and endurance.

C. When we are tested, we must not fail God nor disappoint others who may be inspired by our faith to make spiritual progress (Matt. 5:16).

IV. To Invoke Them to Service

"I shall not die, but live, and declare the works of the Lord" (Ps. 188:17).

A. When they are tested some want to throw up their hands and quit or just lie down and die. They are self-centered, wallowing in self-pity.

10

B. We must accept the challenge when we are tested. God has work for us to do. He may be trying to move us to action.

C. Testing should be used as a stepping, not a stumbling, stone. We must reach out to help the less fortunate, comfort those in sorrow, and share Christ with the unsaved (Phil. 1:12).

5

WHY Christians Can Handle Problems

"But the God of all grace, who hath called us unto his eternal glory by Christ Jesus, after that ye have suffered a while, make you perfect, stablish, strengthen, settle you" (I Peter 5:10).

I. **Work Problems**

"I can do all things through Christ which strengtheneth me" (Phil. 4:13).

A. Christians sometimes have difficulty at their place of employment. They may deny the Lord when they are scoffed at or persecuted for standing up for what is right.

B. We must take our stand for righteousness, but we must take care not to "preach at" fellow workers. God's help is available through prayer and faith for "work problems." "In quietness and in confidence shall be your strength" (Isa. 30:15).

II. **Wallet Problems**

"But my God shall supply all your need according to his riches in glory by Christ Jesus" (Phil. 4:19).

A. Christians have money problems like everyone else. They often fret and figure, but their income just doesn't stretch far enough to meet their needs.

B. We must adjust our living standards to our income, keeping our finances under control.

C. We must also depend on God. When we share with Him first, paying the tithe on our income, we can trust God to multiply the balance and meet our needs (Luke 6:38).

III. **Worry Problems**

"Casting all your care upon him; for he careth for you" (I Peter 5:7).

A. There are two types of Christians—those who are happy and those who are unhappy. Unhappy Christians fail to trust God as they should.

B. We must use our troubles and trials as stepping, not stumbling, stones. God is pleased when His children exhibit carefree, childlike faith.

C. As we help the less fortunate, visit the sick, comfort the bereaved, and share Christ with the unsaved, God will solve our worry problems (Phil. 4:6–8).

IV. **Waiting Problems**

"But let patience have her perfect work, that ye may be perfect and entire, wanting nothing" (James 1:4).

A. Waiting can be the most difficult problem of all; but it often proves to be the most rewarding, for patience teaches faith, and faith pleases God.

B. Faith brings forgiveness, cleansing, healing, miracles, and victory. "And this is the victory that overcometh the world, even our faith" (I John 5:4).

C. When we wait with patience, prayer, perseverance, and purpose, we may be assured that God solves the problem of waiting. "But they that wait upon the Lord shall renew their strength" (Isa. 40:31).

6

WHY Christians Should Be Happy

"Happy is he that hath the God of Jacob for his help, whose hope is in the Lord his God" (Ps. 146:5).

I. They Are Redeemed by the Lord
"...ye were not redeemed with corruptible things, as silver and gold...but with the precious blood of Christ..." (I Peter 1:18–19).
  A. The unredeemed are plagued by guilt. Because they are haunted by feelings of sinfulness and guilt concerning their thoughts, words, and deeds, they cannot be truly happy.
  B. Christians should be happy because their sins are forgiven and their guilt has been removed. They should not allow Satan to destroy their peace of mind and soul with false guilt. "...he is a new creature: old things are passed away" (II Cor. 5:17).

II. They Are Resting in the Lord
"Rest in the Lord, and wait patiently for him: fret not thyself..." (Ps. 37:7).
  A. Many people rush, rush, rush, and wear themselves out. They attempt to carry the responsibility of the world but end up in frustration and misery.
  B. Christians should be happy because they can cast all their care on the Lord (I Peter 5:7). He wants to bear the responsibility for their lives. Christians should do their best and trust the Lord for the rest (Ps. 23:2).

III. Their Refuge Is the Lord
"...He is my refuge and my fortress: my God; in him will I trust" (Ps. 91:2).
  A. Christians are aware of the danger in today's world. They know about the ever-increasing crime rate, the threat of war, the possibility of crippling accidents and deadly diseases.
  B. Christians should also be aware of God's watchful care

and protecting power. They should declare with the psalmist, "The Lord is my light and salvation; whom shall I fear? the Lord is the strength of my life; of whom shall I be afraid?" (Ps. 27:1).

IV. **They Will Reign with the Lord**
"...and they shall reign for ever and ever" (Rev. 22:5).
  A. Christians should be happy because of what God is doing for them here and now, but they should also rejoice over what He has in store for them.
  B. The best is yet to come for Christians. The Lord is preparing an eternal home for them. There they will be reunited with their redeemed loved ones who have gone on before.
  C. Jesus Christ has promised to come again and receive His chosen ones to Himself. They shall reign with Him forever (John 14:1-3).

7

WHY Christians Should Be Like a Tree

"And he shall be like a tree planted by the rivers of water..."
(Ps. 1:3).

I. **A Tree Grows Upward**
"But speaking the truth in love, may grow up into him in all things..." (Eph. 4:15).
  A. A fruit tree is not very useful until it grows upward. Its output of fruit is small. Care and nourishment are needed to hasten its growth.
  B. Christians need to grow upward towards spiritual maturity, bearing the fruits of the Spirit—love, joy, peace, etc. (Gal. 5:22-26).
  C. Christians should be like a tree and grow upward. Prayer, Bible study, and doing God's work will hasten their growth.

II. A Tree Grows Downward

"That Christ may dwell in your hearts by faith; that ye, being rooted and grounded in love, . . ." (Eph. 3:17).

A. Some trees grow as far below the ground surface as they do above it. Storms and winds may bend these trees almost to the ground, but they are unable to uproot and destroy them.

B. Christians need to grow downward also. When strong winds—testing and trial, suffering and sorrow—strike, they must "keep the faith."

C. Christians should be like a tree and grow downward. They must be "rooted and grounded in love" and "stedfast in the faith" (I Peter 5:9–10).

III. A Tree Grows Inward

"But grow in grace, and in the knowledge of our Lord and Saviour Jesus Christ" (II Peter 3:18).

A. The inward growth of trees determines their worth as far as paper products, building materials, etc., are concerned. Those that are inwardly sound and free of decay are the most useful and valuable.

B. Christians need inward growth also. They should grow in grace, understanding, honesty, sincerity, and love. Their inward growth determines their usefulness.

C. Christians, like a tree, should grow inward. Being faithful, trustworthy, and totally committed to God will increase their growth (Eph. 3:16).

IV. A Tree Grows Outward

"Those that be planted in the house of the Lord shall flourish. . . . They shall still bring forth fruit in old age" (Ps. 92:13–14).

A. The outward growth of trees brings to view their beauty and productivity.

B. Christians should grow outward too. They should reach out to help the less fortunate, show kindness and understanding, and witness to the unsaved.

C. Christians, like a tree, should grow outward. Faith, hope, and love will cause their growth to continue and increase (John 15:8).

8

WHY Christians Should Not Be Afraid

"Fear thou not; for I am with thee: be not dismayed; for I am thy God: I will strengthen thee; yea, I will help thee; yea, I will uphold thee with the right hand of my righteousness" (Isa. 41:10).

I. God's Presence Secures
"Fear thou not; for I am with thee..."
- A. Even a child is unafraid when his father is walking beside him, holding his hand. He feels secure because his father is with him.
- B. Christians, our Heavenly Father is with us—at work, play, school, church, everywhere. He is always there, holding our hand. We are secure in His presence (Matt. 14:27).

II. God's Peace Satisfies
"Be not dismayed; for I am thy God..."
- A. Millions are unhappy and discontented. They worship the god of temporal pursuits. Possessions, pleasures, power, and popularity soon decay, depreciate, and deteriorate.
- B. The true and living God satisfies the longing of the soul. Christians should not be dismayed, for God is eternal. All who trust Him as Lord receive peace (Phil. 4:7).

III. God's Power Strengthens
"I will strengthen thee..."
- A. Many Christians run scared because they are not as strong as others. Their lack of physical stamina brings discouragement and failure.
- B. Some of God's spiritual giants have been physical invalids. God's strength is made perfect in weakness (II Cor. 12:9). His power gives strength for the day. We need only to trust and obey (Phil. 4:13).

IV. **God's Provision Supplies**
"Yea, I will help thee..."
   A. Many fail because they try to cope with life's problems on their own. They become frustrated and frightened because prices are high and supplies are low.
   B. God has promised to supply the needs of His children. We shall keep receiving as we keep working, praying, and believing (Phil. 4:19).

V. **God's Promise Sustains**
"Yea, I will uphold thee with the right hand of my righteousness."
   A. The Lord will take His children by the hand and guide them. He will hold them steady in an unsteady world (I Peter 1:5).
   B. God not only sustains His people in this life but has promised to take them to a land where there will be no more sickness, suffering, or sorrow.
   C. Christians should not run scared, for God is with them now and will be with them forever more (I Thess. 4:17).

9

WHY Christians Should Not Worry

"Be careful for nothing; but in every thing by prayer and supplication with thanksgiving let your requests be made known unto God" (Phil. 4:6).

I. **They Have Salvation**
"Receiving the end of your faith, even the salvation of your souls" (I Peter 1:9).
   A. Christians are pardoned. They have repented of their sins and believed on the Lord Jesus Christ. Christians should not worry—they are forgiven and the guilt of sin is removed (Eph. 1:7).
   B. Christians are purified. They have been cleansed from all

sin because they have totally committed their lives to
Jesus Christ (I John 1:7).
  C. The Holy Spirit brings fulfillment to their lives. Chris-
     tians have power for service and purpose for living (Phil.
     4:13).

II. **They Have Serenity**
    "And the peace of God...shall keep your hearts and minds
    through Christ Jesus" (Phil. 4:7).
    A. The world has never sought peace so desperately and
       found so little. Today there is more danger, destruction,
       and devastation than ever before.
    B. Christians should be concerned, pray about these catas-
       trophic conditions, and do what they can to help correct
       them.
    C. Christians have the peace of God and should not worry.
       Through it all—joy and sorrow, sickness and health, life
       and death—they have a deep, settled peace that the
       world cannot give nor take away (John 14:27).

III. **They Have Security**
     "But my God shall supply all your need according to his
     riches in glory by Christ Jesus" (Phil. 4:19).
     A. Many people have materialistic values. They lack secur-
        ity and are trying to find it through the pursuit of money
        and possessions.
     B. Money and possessions alone do not bring happiness and
        security. Christians need not worry because God supplies
        their financial and spiritual needs. "...He satisfieth the
        longing soul" (Ps. 107:9).
     C. Christians can look forward with anticipation to the next
        life. Christ has gone to prepare a place and has promised
        to come again and receive them unto Himself (John
        14:1-3).

IV. **They Give Service**
    "He that believeth on me, the works that I do shall he do
    also" (John 14:12).
    A. Salvation, serenity, and security are God's wonderful
       gifts to us, and we can never sufficiently praise Him
       enough for them.
    B. Receiving is not enough. To stop there brings frustration

and failure. We must give our love, also, if we are to find complete release from worry.

C. We must allow God to do His work through us. When we truly love God, we will love people. Love shares and cares for the less fortunate, the suffering, and bereaved. And it seeks to share Christ with the unsaved (I Cor. 3:9).

10

WHY G-L-O-R-Y Is Due Christ

"And the Word was made flesh, and dwelt among us, (and we beheld his glory, the glory as of the only begotten of the Father,) full of grace and truth" (John 1:14).

I. G-ive
"Who gave himself for us, that he might redeem us from all iniquity..." (Titus 2:14).

A. Christ gave Himself for us. He died on the cross to pay the penalty for our sins. The innocent One died for the guilty.

B. Christ deserves to be glorified in our lives. First, we must accept Him as Lord. We must also share Christ with others and give our tithes and offerings freely and generously. Christ deserves our best—our all (Luke 6:38).

II. L-ove
"...the Son of God, who loved me, and gave himself for me" (Gal. 2:20).

A. Christ's great love brought faith, love, and hope to fallen mankind.

B. Our love brings glory to Christ. When we love Him, we also love the less fortunate, the lonely, the sick, and the bereaved. We bring faith, hope, and love as Christ did (Luke 10:27).

III. O-bey

"...he humbled himself, and became obedient unto death, even the death of the cross" (Phil. 2:8).

A. Christ humbled Himself, becoming "obedient unto death." He was not bound by social pressures but obeyed God rather than men.

B. We bring glory to Christ by following His example of obedience. We obey God when we seek His will and work for Him (Rom. 6:16).

IV. R-ely

"...I do nothing of myself; but as my Father hath taught me, I speak these things" (John 8:28).

A. Christ Himself did not rely on His own power, but He depended on the divine power of His heavenly Father.

B. Neither can we accomplish anything with our own power. We bring glory to Christ by relying on His divine power for daily strength and direction (Prov. 3:5).

V. Y-ield

"O my Father...not as I will, but as thou wilt" (Matt. 26:39).

A. In His most difficult struggle, which involved life or death, Christ chose His Father's will rather than His own human desire. He died to bring life to fallen mankind.

B. When we yield our will to God's will, we become alive in God. We are enabled to work, witness, and win others to Him, bringing glory to Christ (Rom. 6:13).

11

WHY God Allows Trials

"And we know that all things work together for good to them that love God, to them who are the called according to his purpose" (Rom. 8:28).

I. Trials Test Our Faith
"That the trial of your faith...though it be tried with fire, might be found unto praise and honour and glory..." (I Peter 1:7).
   - A. Trials test the caliber of the Christian's faith. By praying and maintaining the proper attitudes, Christians are enabled to make spiritual progress.
   - B. God wants His children to have more faith. We please Him only as we believe (Heb. 11:6).

II. Trials Teach Us Lessons
"...chastened us...for our profit, that we might be partakers of his holiness" (Heb. 12:10).
   - A. When we do not heed God's command, He sometimes allows trials to come our way in order to get our attention.
   - B. We must learn to do those things that are pleasing in God's sight, giving Him first place in our lives. We must learn patience in finding His will and direction for our lives.
   - C. We must learn to have more compassion, understanding, and love for others.

III. Trials Testify to Others
"...afterward it yieldeth the peaceable fruit of righteousness..." (Heb. 12:11).
   - A. Trials testify to others, telling them there is a way through—and that God is the answer to their difficulties.
   - B. As we patiently endure trials, others will be convinced that God can help them in time of trouble.
   - C. When we glorify God through our faith, others will want to put their faith and confidence in Him.

IV. Trials Train for Service

"...every branch that beareth fruit, he purgeth it, that it may bring forth more fruit" (John 15:2).

A. God always has a purpose in what He allows to happen to His children. But everything He allows works together for their good and His glory (Rom. 8:28).

B. After we have experienced trials ourselves, we are better equipped to help others through their struggles. We are better able to assist the less fortunate, to visit the sick, to comfort the bereaved, and to share Christ with the unsaved (Gal. 6:2).

12

WHY It's Great to Be a Christian

"But ye are a chosen generation,...that ye should shew forth the praises of him who hath called you out of darkness into his marvellous light" (I Peter 2:9).

I. A Great Price Is Provided

"For the wages of sin is death; but the gift of God is eternal life through Jesus Christ our Lord" (Rom. 6:23).

A. Mankind sinned, losing fellowship with God through disobedience. Because of his sin man deserved to die, "for the wages of sin is death."

B. It's great to be a Christian because Jesus Christ became our substitute. He gave His life on the cross to pay the penalty for our sins (I Peter 2:24).

C. All who repent and believe receive forgiveness of sins and are restored to fellowship with God.

II. A Great Power Is Possessed

"But ye shall receive power, after that the Holy Ghost is come upon you: and ye shall be witnesses unto me..." (Acts 1:8).

A. The nations of the world are seeking power as never

before. Some want power to protect themselves. Others want power to kill, destroy, and control.

B. Christians need power to do God's work. They are unable to succeed without the help of God.

C. It's great to be a Christian because totally committed Christians are filled with God's love and empowered by the Holy Spirit to work, witness, and win for Him (Phil. 4:13).

III. A Great Peace Is Presented

"...my peace I give unto you.... Let not your heart be troubled, neither let it be afraid" (John 14:27).

A. Today's world is seeking peace through negotiations, threats, and war. But there is more hatred, strife, confusion, and danger than ever before.

B. It's great to be a Christian because Christians can have real and lasting peace in the midst of suffering and sorrow, troubles and trials, desperation and destruction. "And the peace of God...shall keep your hearts and minds through Christ Jesus" (Phil. 4:7).

IV. A Great Prize Is Promised

"In my Father's house are many mansions.... I go to prepare a place for you" (John 14:2).

A. Millions are striving for happiness and security through temporal pursuits. They are selling their souls for pleasure, popularity, and possessions.

B. Temporal things do not bring lasting joy or fill the emptiness and longing of the soul. Even in our affluent society, faith in God is the only way to meet man's inner needs.

C. While salvation brings true contentment and security here and now, the best is yet to come. A great prize is promised—eternal life with Christ in our heavenly home. It's great to be a Christian (John 14:1-3).

13

WHY Jesus Christ Doesn't Change

"Jesus Christ the same yesterday, and to day, and for ever"
(Heb. 13:8).

Introduction: We live in a changing world. Governments and nations, cities and towns, churches and schools, homes and families, and people change, but Jesus Christ never changes.

I. Christ Was the Same Yesterday
"Jesus Christ the same yesterday..."
A. By His omnipotent power God created the heavens and the earth, the beasts, the fish, the fowl. Man, the crown of His creation, was made to have fellowship with God Himself.
B. Man sinned through disobedience and lost fellowship with God. The blood of animals was repeatedly sacrificed to pay the penalty for sins and to bring forgiveness.
C. Jesus Christ loved mankind so much that He paid the penalty for sin once and for all time. With the sacrifice of His own life, He restored man's fellowship with God.
D. Since then, everyone who repents and believes on Christ receives forgiveness of sins. Christ displayed the greatest love possible to mankind (Gal. 2:20).

II. Christ Is the Same Today
"Jesus Christ the same...to day..."
A. Christ's miracle-working power is just as potent today as it was when He created the sun, moon, and stars.
B. Christ's power still brings healing to the sick, comfort to the bereaved, help to the needy, and joy to the sorrowful.
C. Christ's love is just the same today as it was when He died on the cross. Those who come to Him are brought back into fellowship with God.
D. Salvation is available today for all who confess their sins and accept Christ as Saviour and Lord. "...He is faithful and just to forgive...and to cleanse us from all unrighteousness" (I John 1:9).

III. **Christ Will Be the Same Tomorrow**
"Jesus Christ the same... for ever."
  A. Today, perhaps as never before, the future is unknown and uncertain. Many face the unknown with fear, frustration, and some, with fatalism.
  B. Jesus Christ will be the same tomorrow. He will take care of the future if we face it with faith (Rom. 1:17).
  C. We can look forward to the future with anticipation and expectation. Since Christ's love and power will be the same, we may be assured that the best is yet to come.

14

WHY Love Is the Greatest

"And now abideth faith, hope, charity [love], these three; but the greatest of these is charity [love]" (I Cor. 13:13).

I. **Love Feels Compassion**
"Charity [love] suffereth long, and is kind" (I Cor. 13:4).
  A. Many Christians do not feel compassion for others as they should. More of God's love is needed. Love elicits compassion.
  B. We receive more love by recognizing our need for love and asking God to supply it. We cannot love another and carry ill feelings toward him at the same time.
  C. Love drives away resentments and replaces them with compassion. Love is the greatest.

II. **Love Gives Comfort**
"...seeketh not her own... thinketh no evil" (I Cor. 13:5).
  A. Some Christians are self-centered, caring only for their own comfort. Their first thoughts are concerned with, "How will this affect me?"
  B. Love cares about and seeks to bring comfort to others. Love is willing to sacrifice. It goes out of its way to help the less fortunate.

When we are filled with God's love, giving comfort to others brings fulfillment to us. Love is the greatest.

Love Shares Concern

"Rejoiceth not in iniquity, but rejoiceth in the truth" (I Cor. 13:6).

A. Sometimes Christians secretly rejoice about the misfortunes of others. They lack love and are selfishly concerned about their personal gain.

B. The misfortunes of others bring pain and sorrow to those who love. They seek ways and means to help and share with those in need.

C. Love is also concerned about the spiritual needs of others. It shares Christ with the unsaved and seeks to bring them to forgiveness and cleansing (I John 1:9). Love is the greatest.

IV. Love Always Conquers

"Charity [love] never faileth" (I Cor. 13:8).

A. Possessions, pleasure, popularity, and personal pursuits often bring disappointment. They are temporal and do not give lasting satisfaction.

B. Friends sometimes fail. Loved ones may bring hurt and misunderstanding. Although we are subject to human frailties, we must continue to love.

C. Love never fails. There is no defense against love. It always wins. Love brings victory here and now. Love will reign eternally in the life to come. It always conquers (I Cor. 13:13). Love is the greatest.

15

WHY Not Expect a Miracle?

"Jesus of Nazareth, a man approved of God among you by miracles..." (Acts 2:22).

I. Pray
"...men ought always to pray, and not to faint" (Luke 18:1).

A. Everything that concerns our lives should begin with prayer. Prayer will bring victory in time of battle.

B. God often allows trials to come to His children to get their attention. He wants to teach them lessons and lead them to higher heights and deeper depths.

C. Are you in difficulty? Pray about it. Are you going through deep water? Through the fire? Pray about it.

D. Are you in the valley of affliction? Do you need a miracle? Pray about it. God answers prayer. "Pray without ceasing" (I Thess. 5:17).

II. Believe
"...all things are possible to him that believeth" (Mark 9:23).

A. To be effective our prayers are sometimes delayed so that we must use our faith.

B. Many want to see the miracle first and then they will believe. But we must believe first and then we shall receive.

C. God often allows Christians to encounter situations that require faith. Faith increases as we use what we have.

D. Like everyone else Christians are subjected to testing and trial, but faith makes the difference. "...According to your faith be it unto you" (Matt. 9:29).

III. Work
"Even so faith, if it hath not works, is dead, being alone" (James 2:17).

A. Many people are in difficulty and need a miracle. They

pray, but nothing happens. They are frustrated and disappointed.

B. To be effective, prayer and faith must be accompanied by action. Positive action activates our faith and brings success (James 2:22).

C. We must earnestly pray about our needs, sincerely believe that God will take care of us, and then do what we can to help bring miracles to pass.

D. Miracles do happen; needs are supplied; and victory is assured to those who pray, believe, and work.

16

WHY Not Overcome Frustrations?

"But the God of all grace, who hath called us unto his eternal glory by Christ Jesus, after that ye have suffered a while, make you perfect, stablish, strengthen, settle you" (I Peter 5:10).

I. Delay Action on Big Decisions

"Wait on the Lord...wait, I say, on the Lord" (Ps. 27:14).

A. Many make rash decisions. They take quick action when they don't know what to do. Their errors in judgment often add to their distress and frustration.

B. When we don't know which way to turn, we should delay making decisions which could affect or change the direction of our life.

C. We must wait on the Lord until we get a right perspective. Then we can move forward with confidence, assured of God's direction. "In your patience possess ye your souls" (Luke 21:19).

II. Devote More Time to Devotions

"Draw nigh to God, and he will draw nigh to you" (James 4:8).

A. Many people become so engulfed trying to solve their problems that they neglect to pray. Neglect brings failure.

B. When we do not know which course of action to take, we must petition God, heed His Word, and wait for His time.

C. Direction is found through prayer, patience, and perseverance (I Thess. 5:17–18).

III. Do God's Work Diligently

"We then, as workers together with him..." (II Cor. 6:1).

A. Not knowing which way to turn doesn't mean that we are to sit with folded hands and do nothing. This will only add to our indecision and confusion.

B. While we should delay acting on big decisions and give more time to devotions, we must not stop there. We must do something for God.

C. Lending a helping hand to the less fortunate, visiting the sick and elderly, attending church faithfully, and sharing Christ with others will help bring direction to your life (II Thess. 2:17).

IV. Depend on God for Direction

"In all thy ways acknowledge him, and he shall direct thy paths" (Prov. 3:6).

A. All too many Christians depend on themselves too much. Failure to trust in the Lord brings defeat.

B. When we don't know which way to turn, we must put our faith and confidence in God, depending on His direction.

C. We must believe that God is alive and is concerned about us. We can be assured that "greater is he that is in you, than he that is in the world" (I John 4:4). Depending on God brings guidance and the healing of frustration.

17

WHY Some Christians Backslide

"But seek ye first the kingdom of God, and his righteousness; and all these things shall be added unto you" (Matt. 6:33).

I. Lack of Prayer
"...men ought always to pray, and not to faint" (Luke 18:1).

A. Many Christians are defeated because they fail to pray as they should. Some become too busy with temporal pursuits and neglect their prayer life.

B. Others become so busy doing God's work that they neglect to pray.

C. We must take and make time to pray. Prayer is our means of communication and fellowship with God. It solves problems and supplies needs (Matt. 26:41).

II. Lure of Pleasure
"Ye have lived in pleasure on the earth, and been wanton" (James 5:5).

A. We live in a pleasure-mad world. Many are seeking pleasure at any cost—illicit sex, perversions, drunkenness, drug abuse, etc.

B. Some are sacrificing their home, marriage, family, love, and life for sinful and fleeting pleasures.

C. Christians must not be deceived by the lure of sinful pleasure. We must give God first place in our lives and keep our values in perspective.

III. Love of Possessions
"...a man's life consisteth not in the abundance of the things which he possesseth" (Luke 12:15).

A. Our affluent society has brought spiritual poverty to millions. Many have devoted their life and labor to attaining earthly rather than heavenly treasures.

B. Christians who get caught up in aspirations for money, houses, land, cars, boats, and gadgets often neglect Christ and fall into temptation.

C. We must set our "affection on things above, not on things on the earth" (Col. 3:2). Loving God and others, assisting the poor, and sharing Christ bring spiritual wealth.

IV. **Lust for Popularity**

"Looking unto Jesus the author and finisher of our faith" (Heb. 12:2).

A. Many Christians become cynical because they center their attention on the faults and failures of others. Some lean on other people and become too dependent on them.

B. Too many Christians seek the approval of others. They go to any extreme to get honor and applause from men.

C. We must not lust for popularity. We gain spiritual insight when we keep our eyes on Jesus. He is the only one who never fails nor forsakes (John 5:44).

18

WHY Tears Are of Value

"Jesus wept" (John 11:35).

I. **Tears of Confession**

"And Peter remembered the word of Jesus. . . . And he went out, and wept bitterly" (Matt. 26:75).

A. Peter denied Christ. He was ashamed to be counted as one of His disciples when the pressure was on. But when Peter wept bitterly in confession and repentance, he was forgiven and spiritually restored.

B. We must never allow social pressures to keep us from taking our stand for Christ or cause us to be ashamed of Him.

C. For those who have rejected or failed Christ, tears of confession and repentance, with faith, are needed to bring forgiveness and restoration (I John 1:9).

31

Lou Holtz Story

II. Tears of Commitment

"Serving the Lord with all humility of mind, and with many tears..." (Acts 20:19).

A. Paul was totally committed to Christ. No sacrifice was too great. No burden, too heavy. No task, too difficult. No affliction, too severe. With tears of consecration he served the Lord humbly and finished his course with joy (Acts 20:24).

B. If we are totally committed to Christ, the Holy Spirit will enable us to do God's work. We will help the needy, comfort the bereaved, and witness to the lost with joy.

III. Tears of Compassion

"...He beheld the city, and wept over it" (Luke 19:41).

Little Girl Helping

A. Jesus had great compassion. He was concerned about the sinful. He cared for the sick. He comforted those in sorrow. He wept with compassion because He loved.

B. We must also love others. Tears of compassion will heal hurts, remove resentments, soothe strifes, and conquer conflicts.

C. There is no defense against love. We should love with tears of compassion as Jesus did. He cared so much that He died for us (Gal. 2:20).

IV. Tears of Conquest

"They that sow in tears shall reap in joy" (Ps. 126:5).

A. Christians may not always have an easy life in today's troubled world. Sometimes there are mountains to climb, valleys to descend, and rivers to cross.

B. We must give God first place and do those things faithfully that bring glory to Him. If at times we have to "sow in tears," we "shall reap in joy."

C. Christians can be conquerors even in this life. But the best is yet to come. Eternal life with the Lord awaits the faithful. Heaven is a place where tears will be unknown. "And God shall wipe away all tears from their eyes... for the former things are passed away" (Rev. 21:4).

19

WHY There's Power in the Gospel

"For I am not ashamed of the gospel of Christ: for it is the power of God unto salvation to every one that believeth" (Rom. 1:16).

I. To Save
"... unto us which are saved it is the power of God" (I Cor. 1:18).
A. Man is powerless to save himself. Good deeds, good morals, going to church, and giving to the church will not suffice.
B. One can be saved only through the power of God. When we call on the name of the Lord, confess our sins, repent, and believe, we receive complete forgiveness (Rom. 10:13).

II. To Sanctify
"Sanctify them through thy truth: thy word is truth" (John 17:17).
A. Christians cannot rid themselves of greed, jealousy, resentment, and strife through their own strength. They must depend on the power of God.
B. When we totally surrender ourselves to God, His Holy Spirit cleanses our whole spirit and fills us with His divine love (I Thess. 5:23).

III. To Satisfy
"For he satisfieth the longing soul, and filleth the hungry soul with goodness" (Ps. 107:9).
A. In today's affluent society people are more discontented, miserable, and unhappy than ever before.
B. We must submit to the power of the gospel if we are to find real joy and contentment. God's power solves problems, lifts burdens, mends broken homes, and brings peace and satisfaction to troubled minds and souls (Phil. 4:7).

IV. To Stabilize

"Who are kept by the power of God through faith..." (I Peter 1:5).

A. Many desire Christ as Saviour but fear they cannot live the Christian life. Many Christians lack stability because their commitment to Christ is not complete.

B. No one can be a faithful Christian within his own strength. We must depend on the power of God. "But the God of all grace...stablish, strengthen, settle you" (I Peter 5:10).

V. For Service

"But ye shall receive power, after that the Holy Ghost is come upon you: and ye shall be witnesses unto me..." (Acts 1:8).

A. Many Christians attend church, pay tithes, and give offerings, but their service to God stops there. They are unconcerned, fearful, and perhaps too lazy to do more.

B. God's power enables totally committed Christians to do His work. They assist the needy, visit the sick, comfort the bereaved, work in God's house, and share Christ with others (II Cor. 6:1).

20

WHY We Need a Right Perspective

"Looking unto Jesus the author and finisher of our faith" (Heb. 12:2).

I. About People

"And thou shalt love the Lord thy God with all thy heart, and with all thy soul, and with all thy mind, and with all thy strength.... Thou shalt love thy neighbor as thyself."

A. Many lack a right perspective where others are concerned. Some hold ill feelings and resentments. Some depend too much on others—ministers, doctors, friends, or loved ones; they rely on them instead of the Lord.

B. God must have first place in our lives. We should love others and appreciate the assistance and kindness we receive from them, but we must put our ultimate faith and trust in God. He never fails (Ps. 118:8-9).

II. About Problems

"Casting all your care upon him; for he careth for you" (I Peter 5:7).

A. Many people are engulfed by their problems. They work with their problems, bring them home, and eat and sleep with them. Their lives are frustrated and exhausted with problems.

B. We must face up to our problems, recognizing them for what they are, and seek solutions for them. Our faith and God's help can bring a right perspective. We must trust the Lord implicitly, for He is able to solve our problems for us (Ps. 62:8).

III. About Possessions

". . . a man's life consisteth not in the abundance of the things which he possesseth" (Luke 12:15).

A. In today's affluent society, millions are overly concerned about materialistic pursuits. The more they get, the more they want. They are seeking security in possessions.

B. Material things do not bring lasting security or happiness. They wear out, rust out, and deteriorate. While a reasonable amount of money is necessary, spiritual things remain most important.

C. Getting a right perspective involves our stewardship—helping the needy, comforting the bereaved, and sharing Christ with the lost. Spiritual things are of eternal value (John 6:27).

IV. About Possibilities

". . . with God all things are possible" (Matt. 19:26).
". . . all things are possible to him that believeth" (Mark 9:23).

A. Many people are pessimistic. They see only the drab, dark, and dreary side of life. They are unfulfilled and unhappy.

B. We must look for the good and try to improve on the bad.

Everyone can do something for God if he tries. Each can smile, make a call, lend a helping hand.
C. Having a right perspective brings help for this life and hope for the next. With a positive outlook and outreach, the best is yet to come (John 14:1-3).

21

WHY We Need an Understanding Heart

"Give therefore thy servant an understanding heart to judge thy people, that I may discern between good and bad: for who is able to judge this thy so great a people?" (I Kings 3:9).

I. **Understanding Inspires Loyalty**
"But the Lord is faithful, who shall stablish you, and keep you from evil" (II Thess. 3:3).
A. The Lord is faithful and loyal. He is friend, helper, and Saviour. He never fails nor forsakes any who come to Him. He understands.
B. An understanding heart will help us to be loyal and trustworthy also. We will not be ashamed of Christ nor betray the confidence of others.
C. Those who are faithful unto death will receive a crown of life in the hereafter (Rev. 2:10).

II. **Understanding Involves Listening**
"The righteous cry, and the Lord heareth, and delivereth them out of all their troubles" (Ps. 34:17).
A. The understanding Christ always listens to those who call on Him. He never turns a deaf ear to any problem or need (Ps. 91:15).
B. We must listen to Him as He speaks to us through prayer and His Word.
C. We must listen to others too. In our world of suffering, sorrow, and separation, listening can make the difference between life and death. An understanding heart lends a listening ear.

III. Understanding Invests Labor

"...the poor have the gospel preached to them" (Matt. 11:5).

A. Jesus Christ listens to our troubles, but He also lifts our burdens and delivers us out of our troubles.

B. An understanding heart must lend a helping hand as well as a listening ear. We must put feet to our prayers and works to our faith.

C. We must help the poor and disabled, visit and pray for the sick, assist in the work of the church, and seek to give the gospel to the poor (James 2:14–24).

IV. Understanding Increases Love

"...the Son of God, who loved me, and gave himself for me" (Gal. 2:20).

A. The understanding Jesus is filled with compassion and love. He loved so much that He died on the cross to pay the penalty for our sins.

B. Loyalty, listening, and labor are necessary to an understanding heart, but without love they fall short of their potential (I Cor. 13:1–3).

C. An understanding heart increases love. God's love enables us to feel compassion and empathize with others in their deepest needs. Love will bring final victory with its eternal rewards at the coming of our Lord Jesus Christ (I Thess. 3:12–13).

22

WHY We Need Faith

"And this is the victory that overcometh the world, even our faith" (I John 5:4).

I. **Faith Dissolves Doubts**

"Now faith is...the evidence of things not seen" (Heb. 11:1).

   A. Many Christians are doubters. They approach almost every situation with a negative and pessimistic attitude. They usually fail, for doubters seldom succeed.

   B. Faith is optimistic. It looks for the good and expects the best. Faith assures us that everything works together for our good (Rom. 8:28).

   C. We must have faith. Faith crowds out doubts and brings victory over them.

II. **Faith Dispels Dread**

"Be not afraid, only believe" (Mark 5:36).

   A. In today's world many are fearful about the future. They fear the possibility of atomic confrontation. They dread financial loss, failing health, growing old, etc.

   B. Faith doesn't dispose of the awareness of these possibilities, but it dispels the fear and dread of them.

   C. Christians know that a faith that can calm a raging, rolling sea can also bring peace to the disturbed, disquieted hearts and minds of those who trust in God (Mark 4:40).

III. **Faith Disarms Defeat**

"...all things are possible to him that believeth" (Mark 9:23).

   A. Many Christians give up too easily. They lack the faith to keep holding on when answers are delayed and results are slow coming in.

   B. Faith is never defeated, although there may be delays. Christians must wait for God's time and way.

   C. We fight the good fight of faith by doing God's work— helping the needy, encouraging the disheartened, and sharing Christ with the lost. There is no defeat for those who keep on believing (I John 5:4).

IV. **Faith Destroys Death**

"The last enemy that shall be destroyed is death" (I Cor. 15:26).

A. There is no eternal death for those who repent of their sins. Faith in the Lord Jesus Christ destroys eternal death (John 3:16).

B. When Christians accept Christ as Saviour and Lord of their lives, they need not fear death. "And whosoever liveth and believeth in me shall never die" (John 11:26).

C. Faith assures us of eternal life, not death. In heaven there will be no more physical death, neither sorrow, crying, or pain. "For the former things are passed away" (Rev. 21:4).

23

WHY We Need the Holy S-P-I-R-I-T

"The Spirit itself beareth witness with our spirit, that we are the children of God" (Rom. 8:16).

I. **S-aves**

"Repent ye... that your sins may be blotted out, when the times of refreshing shall come..." (Acts 3:19).

A. After Christ died on the cross for our sins, He ascended to heaven and sent His Holy Spirit to earth.

B. All who repent and believe may receive forgiveness of sins. Jesus Christ saves through the work of the Holy Spirit (Eph. 2:8).

II. **P-urifies**

"... giving them the Holy Ghost... purifying their hearts by faith" (Acts 15:8–9).

A. The Holy Spirit purifies the hearts of Christians who totally commit themselves to Him.

B. Purified Christians are filled with the love of God and empowered for service by the Holy Spirit (Acts 1:8).

III. I-nstructs

"...the Holy Ghost...shall teach you all things..." (John 14:26).

A. Many Christians lack understanding, direction, and the assurance of God's presence in their lives. They are frustrated and often fail.

B. Christians find needed direction by depending on the enlightenment of the Holy Spirit. He also instructs them in the deeper truths of God (John 16:13).

IV. R-evives

"But ye shall receive power, after that the Holy Ghost is come upon you: and ye shall be witnesses unto me..." (Acts 1:8).

A. Many weak Christians fail when it comes to doing God's work.

B. They need the power of the Holy Spirit. The Holy Spirit enables totally committed Christians to work, witness, and win others to Jesus Christ (Rom. 8:11).

V. I-ndwells

"...he shall give you another Comforter, that he may abide with you for ever" (John 14:16).

A. The Holy Spirit comes into the heart and life of the completely surrendered Christian to comfort and abide with him forever.

B. He gives surrendered Christians God's love, enabling them to reach out to help, comfort, and love others (John 14:23).

VI. T-ouches

"And he took him by the right hand, and lifted him up..." (Acts 3:7).

A. The Holy Spirit heals through doctors, medicine, and by His direct touch.

B. We need the Holy Spirit to touch us physically, mentally, and spiritually. He works in accordance with God's will and our faith (Matt. 9:29).

24

WHY We Should Be H-O-L-Y

"...it is written, Be ye holy; for I am holy" (I Peter 1:16).

I. H-umble

"And being found in fashion as a man, he humbled himself..." (Phil. 2:8).

A. Jesus Christ the Son of God came down from the splendors of heaven and humbled Himself, becoming "in fashion as a man."

B. Christ was not affected by sinful pride or social pressures but lived to help others. He humbled Himself in order to pay the penalty for the sins of mankind.

C. Humility is concurrent with holiness. We must be willing to do the small and thankless tasks. We must follow the example of Christ, who was loving and forgiving (I Peter 5:6).

II. O-bedient

"...and became obedient unto death, even the death of the cross" (Phil. 2:8).

A. Christ was obedient to His Father. He wanted to please Him in everything He did.

B. Many Christians know what they should do for Christ, but they fail. They are pursuing personal pleasures and possessions.

C. If we are to obey the command to be holy, we must be as Christ was. We must take time for God and give Him first place in our lives (Matt. 6:33).

III. L-oving

"...that the love wherewith thou hast loved me may be in them, and I in them" (John 17:26).

A. Jesus loved His enemies as well as His friends. He loved so much that He gave His life for all mankind.

B. We must love as Jesus did. We must pray for, forgive, and love those who hurt, disappoint, and misunderstand.

C. We cannot be holy unless we love God and others. Love

reaches out to help the helpless, give hope to the hopeless, and share Christ with those who do not know Him (I John 4:11).

IV. Y-ielded
"Nevertheless not my will, but thine, be done" (Luke 22:42).
A. When the most critical testing came to Christ—a matter of life and death—He yielded His will to His Father's will.
B. God's will is best for us even in times of trouble, testing, and trial (Rom. 8:28).
C. Holiness means that the Christian is totally committed to God's will. Yielding to God's will enables us to work and witness here in this life, and it brings the assurance of everlasting life in the hereafter (Rom. 6:22).

25

WHY We Should Make Spiritual Progress

"...let us lay aside every weight, and the sin which doth so easily beset us, and let us run with patience the race that is set before us" (Heb. 12:1).

I. We Think
"For as he thinketh in his heart, so is he" (Prov. 23:7).
A. Many dwell on the negative side. Their pessimism brings disappointment to themselves, discouragement to others, and displeasure to God.
B. We must think positively, crowding out negativism with thoughts of faith, hope, and love (Phil. 4:8).

II. We See
"Looking unto Jesus the author and finisher of our faith" (Heb. 12:2).
A. Our world is filled with sin, suffering, and sorrow. Many become bitter because they see only the faults and failures in others.

B. Love covers the multitude of sins (I Peter 4:8). We can be a blessing only by looking for the good in others and keeping our eyes on Jesus.

III. We Hear

"...He that heareth...and believeth...hath everlasting life..." (John 5:24).

A. Television and radio communicate sensualism, smut, and slander. These weaken the Christian faith.

B. We must listen to the voice of God. We must hear the cries of the needy, the frustrated, and the lost, and seek to bring them to a saving knowledge of Jesus Christ.

IV. We Speak

"For by thy words thou shalt be justified, and by thy words thou shalt be condemned" (Matt. 12:37).

A. Many speak unkindly to others. Their critical and thoughtless words bring them into condemnation.

B. We must speak words of comfort, encouragement, and understanding, sharing Christ with the unsaved when opportunity affords.

V. We Do

"...that they be rich in good works...that they may lay hold on eternal life" (I Tim. 6:18-19).

A. Many are self-centered, concerned only with selfish pursuits and personal gain.

B. Christians should be engaged in the service of the Lord. Helping the needy, visiting the sick, comforting the bereaved, and witnessing to the lost bring assurance of eternal life.

VI. We Go

"In my Father's house are many mansions...I will come again, and receive you unto myself" (John 14:2-3).

A. God's Word teaches that there is a heaven to gain and a hell to shun. Eternal destruction awaits those who reject Christ.

B. Eternal life and the joys of heaven await those who repent and accept Christ as Saviour and Lord. We are all going somewhere. Where are you going?

26

WHY You Can Win over Temptation

"There hath no temptation taken you but such as is common to man: but God is faithful, who will not suffer you to be tempted above that ye are able; but will with the temptation also make a way to escape, that ye may be able to bear it" (I Cor. 10:13).

I. Satan Presents the Test

"There hath no temptation taken you but such as is common to man."

A. Every Christian is subjected to temptation. It isn't sinful to be tempted. Temptation is "common to man."

B. Christians should stay as far away from Satan's territory as possible. They spare themselves many temptations by doing so.

C. Satan tempts through the mind. He tempts through the desire for temporal possessions, for power, and for sexual gratification. Temptation does not become sinful lust unless one yields to the temptation (Rom. 6:12–13).

D. Christ was tempted in every way, but He did not yield to sin. He is our example. We must not yield to temptation but overcome as He did (Heb. 4:15).

II. You Perform the Best

"But God is faithful, who will not suffer you to be tempted above that ye are able."

A. Many Christians fail to perform their best. They want to see how near to sinful pursuits and practices they can get and still remain a Christian.

B. In our quest for victory we must constantly do our very best to overcome the attacks of Satan. "Resist the devil, and he will flee from you" (James 4:7).

C. If we draw near to God, He will draw near to us (James 4:8). We can also defeat Satan through prayer and quoting God's Word as Christ did. "Satan, get thee hence," said Jesus.

D. God requires no more of His children than they "are

able" to bear. We may be assured if we "perform the best," God will "provide the rest."

III. **God Provides the Rest**
"But will with the temptation also make a way to escape, that ye may be able to bear it."
A. When Satan strikes, Christians must do their best to resist him.
B. Satan is subtle, deceiving "the very elect" if possible (Matt. 24:24). But God has promised to "make a way to escape" and enable us to triumph through Him who loves us (Rom. 8:37).
C. Satan presents testings, temptations, troubles, and trials, but Christians must keep on working, praying, trusting, and believing God's Word. They can conquer through God's help (II Cor. 3:5).
D. When we have performed our best, God will provide the rest—not only in this life but He offers eternal rest in the life to come (Heb. 4:9).

27

WHY You Should Be Aware of Sin

"For the wages of sin is death; but the gift of God is eternal life through Jesus Christ our Lord" (Rom. 6:23).

I. **The Pleasure of Sin**
"Choosing rather to suffer affliction with the people of God, than to enjoy the pleasures of sin for a season" (Heb. 11:25).
A. Millions are captivated by the pleasures of sin. They sell their souls for fleeting moments of sinful pleasure.
B. Satan presents only the attractive side of sin. He pictures the alluring glitter and passing fancies that sin offers (James 5:5).

II. The Pitfalls of Sin

"But every man is tempted, when he is drawn away of his own lust, and enticed" (James 1:14).

A. Sin involves many pitfalls which lead to the downfall and destruction of body, mind, and soul. Drug abuse, alcoholism, and illicit sex are examples.

B. Unsuspecting souls who try to hold to God with one hand and to Satan with the other unwittingly fall into Satan's snare and may become trapped in the pitfalls of sin (II Tim. 2:26).

III. The Progression of Sin

"Then when lust hath conceived, it bringeth forth sin" (James 1:15).

A. Satan is deceptive. He works through the love of money, the lure of sinful pleasure, and the lusts of the flesh. He will deceive the very elect if possible. He is never satisfied.

B. Sin doesn't stop with desire and pleasure but keeps driving forward until it finally destroys the soul of its victim. Sin is progressive (II Tim. 3:13).

IV. The Penalty of Sin

"And sin, when it is finished, bringeth forth death" (James 1:15).

A. Before the fall of mankind God placed the penalty of death on the sin of disobedience (Gen. 2:17).

B. The penalty of death for sin has never been removed. It is still in effect. All who continue to live in sin are doomed to hell and eternal death (Rom. 6:23).

V. The Pardon for Sin

"If we confess our sins, he is faithful and just to forgive us our sins, and to cleanse us from all unrighteousness" (I John 1:9).

A. Pardon is available. We need not pay the penalty of death. Christ paid it for us by dying on the cross for our sins (Titus 2:14).

B. We can repent of our sins and receive forgiveness for them. We can totally commit our lives to Christ and be cleansed from all sin (I John 1:7).

28

WHY You Should Believe in Miracles

"Jesus of Nazareth, a man approved of God among you by miracles and wonders and signs, which God did by him in the midst of you..." (Acts 2:22).

I. Remember Past Miracles
"The Lord hath done great things for us" (Ps. 126:3).
   A. The disciples, in the midst of the wind-tossed sea, were troubled and frightened when they saw Jesus walking on the water. "For they considered not the miracle of the loaves" (Mark 6:52).
   B. Many Christians today who are going through troubled waters have forgotten how God helped, healed, or delivered them in the past.
   C. We need to recall past miracles and praise the Lord for them. Recounting them will also bless others, glorify God, and bring His assurance: "Be of good cheer: it is I; be not afraid" (Mark 6:50).

II. Recognize Present Miracles
"This is the Lord's doing, and it is marvellous in our eyes..." (Matt. 21:42).
   A. Many Christians are too involved in temporal pursuits. Some are so busy looking and praying for miracles that they fail to recognize them when they happen.
   B. Miracles happen to Christians who expect to receive them. Ignoring the blessings of God brings defeat to ourselves, discouragement to others, and displeasure to God (Heb. 11:6).
   C. We should recognize God's miracles daily. Write them down. List them one by one. We are forgiven, cleansed, and good things are happening. Recognizing our blessings brings a positive attitude, enabling us to reach out to help and share Christ with others.

III. Rejoice about Potential Miracles

"Be glad and rejoice: for the Lord will do great things" (Joel 2:21).

A. When we recall past miracles and recognize present ones, we activate our faith, making it easier to believe that God will keep right on blessing us. "Jesus Christ the same yesterday, and to day, and for ever" (Heb. 13:8).

B. We must not only praise God for past and present miracles, but we must also rejoice for the ones which are to come. Rejoicing triggers our faith. Faith pleases God, bringing continued blessings (I John 5:4).

C. God's greatest miracle is salvation through Jesus Christ. Salvation brings eternal life. Eternal life leads to a home in heaven, the greatest miracle of all (John 14:1-3).